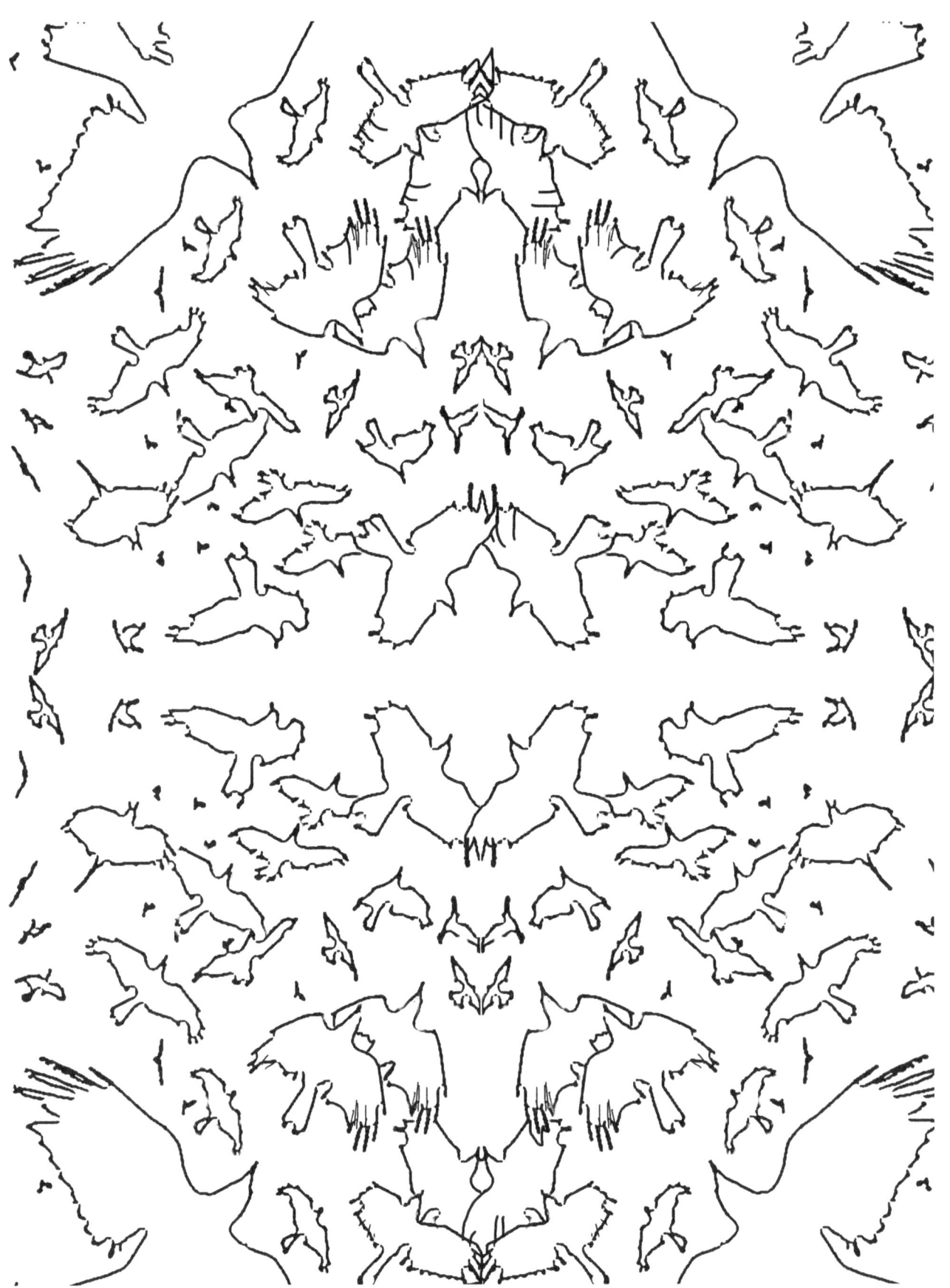

AUTHOR AND ILLUSTRATOR, JOSEPH RICE'S PREVIOUS WORK INCLUDES MURALS, SET DESIGN, BOOK ILLUSTRATION

IN THIS BOOK ANCIENT BRITISH THEMES AND IMAGERY FILL THE PAGES. THE INSPIRATION COMES FROM INSTANTLY RECOGNISABLE DESIGNS THAT HAVE GRACED THESE ISLANDS FOR MILLENNIA.

FROM THE NEOLITHIC, CELTIC AND ANGLO-SAXON BRITAIN THE DISTINCTIVE STYLE OF INTERWEAVING DESIGNS REMAINED CONSTANT RIGHT UP TO THE NORMAN CONQUEST. WITH THE EXCEPTION OF THE ROMAN OCCUPATION, THIS IS THE LONGEST PERIOD OF THE INDIGENOUS DESIGNS ASSOCIATED WITH THE BRITISH ISLES. ALSO THE STRONG SCANDINAVIAN INFLUENCES AS DEPICTED BY BEOWULF CONFRONTING GRENDLE 13-14

THE DESIGNS USED FOR HEREWARD THE WAKE'S ILLUSTRATION ARE BASED UPON HELMET DECORATIONS FROM THE STAFFORDSHIRE HOARD AND THE BURIAL GOODS UNEARTHED AT SUTTON HOO

HEREWARD LED ARMED RESISTANCE AGAINST THE NORMAN INVADERS AS THEY ATTEMPTED TO EXPAND THEIR CONTROL OVER MORE AND MORE OF ENGLAND. AS A CHRISTIAN THE DECORATIONS AND EMBLEMS WOULD HAVE BEEN FAR LESS PAGAN THAN THE EXAMPLES I USED AS A RESOURCE, BUT THE FORMAL STYLE WOULD HAVE BEEN RECOGNISABLE AS THE HELMET DESIGNS HAD EVOLVED GRADUALLY DURING THE 500 OR SO YEARS IN WHICH ANGLO SAXON BRITAIN EMERGED FROM THE DARK AGES OF POST ROMAN BRITAIN.

Colouring in with Complimentary colours

In the colour wheel, the primary colours point to their opposites or complimentary colours.

When placed together they contrast. By using a green in its pure state next to a green with a hint of its complimentary colour added to it, it is possible to make both greens contrast slightly, which adds vibrancy to the work. This works better with pure or process colours. Experiment, each colour can have six extra shades when mixed with primary and secondary colours

PRIMARY COLOURS
RED, YELLOW & BLUE
THESE CANNOT BE MADE BY MIXING
COLOURS TOGETHER

SECONDARY COLOURS
ORANGE, GREEN &
PURPLE
ARE MADE BY MIXING PRIMARY
COLOURS

THE GRAND ORDER
OF
ARIAL STEAM NAVIGATORS

PRESENTS

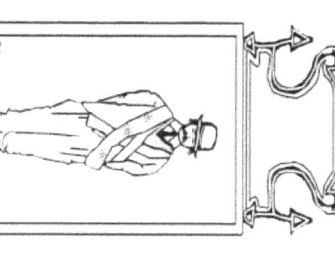

JOSEPH RICE'S HARD COLOURING
BOOK FOR GROWN-UPS
ANCIENT BRITISH THEMES AND
DESIGNS TO COLOUR IN

NEXT
BOOK:
"DREAMS
OF STEAM"

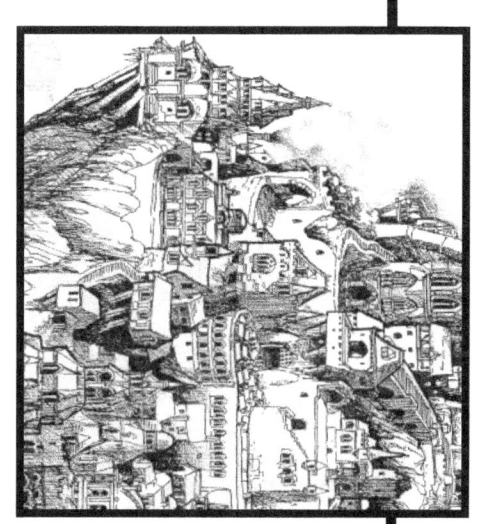

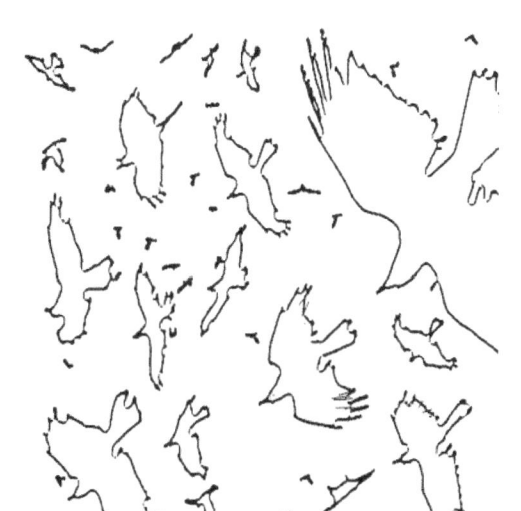

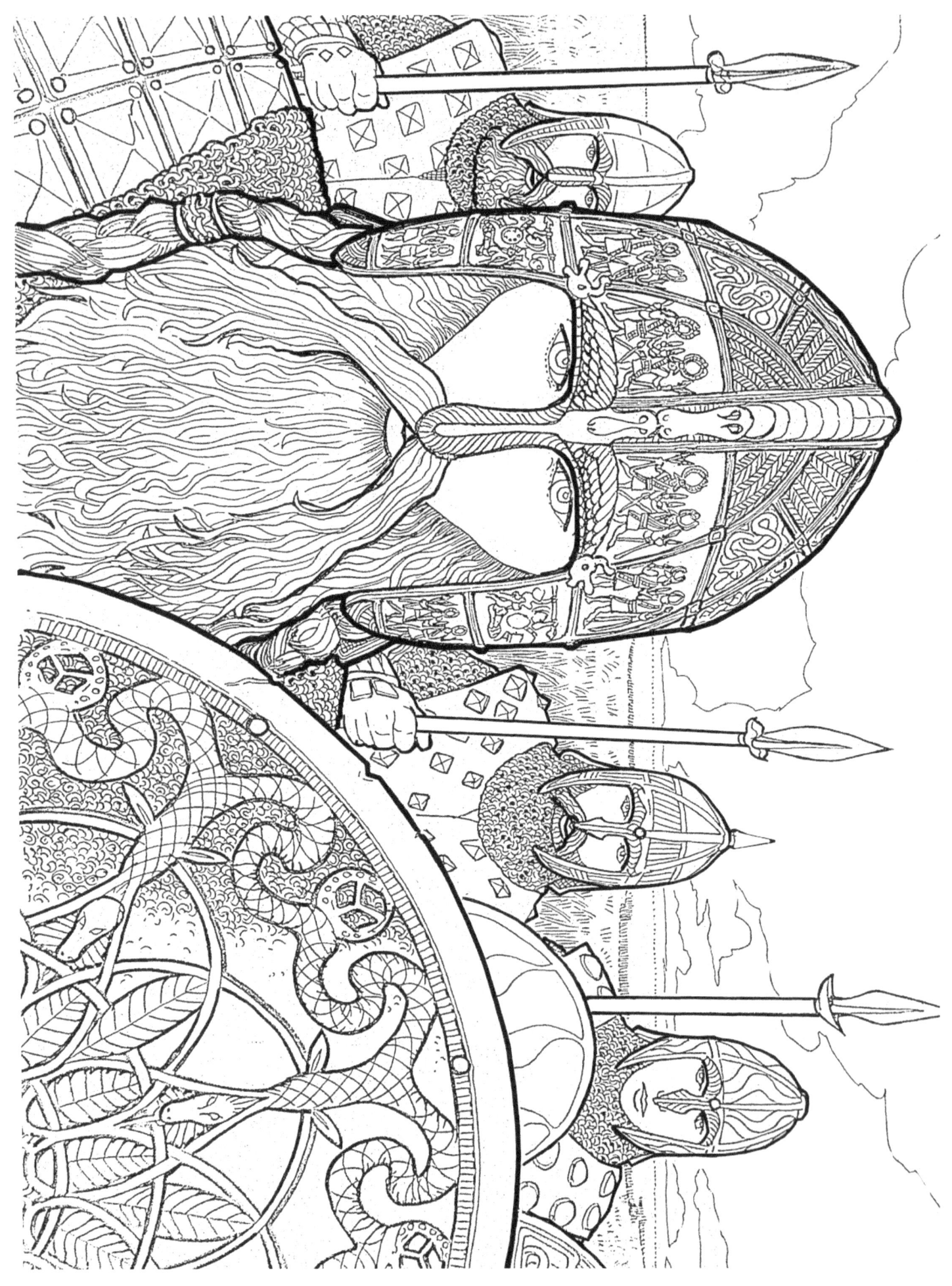

HEREWARD THE WAKE

SAXON RESISTANCE LEADER, WHO OPPOSED THE NORMAN'S MILITARY EXPANSION AFTER 1066

HEREWARD IS DEPICTED WITH THE CLASSIC ANGLO SAXON SHIELD AND HELM, BASED ON THE DESIGN OF ARTIFACTS FOUND AT THE STAFFORDSHIRE HOARD AND SUTTON HOO BURIAL GOODS.

STYLES OF DECORATION EVOLVED OVER TIME, WITH CHRISTIAN ICONOGRAPHY SUBSUMING THE EARLIER PAGAN IMAGERY .

HEREWARD AND HIS FOLLOWERS ARE SHOWN IN REEDY FENLAND WHERE HIS CAM-PAIGNS TOOK PLACE, IN WHAT IS NOW CAMBRIDGESHIRE

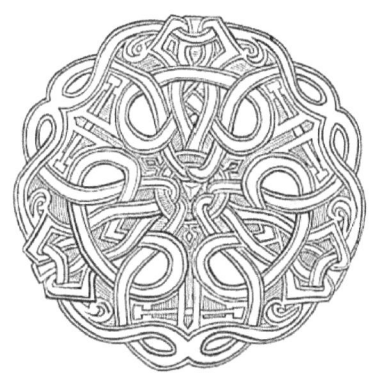

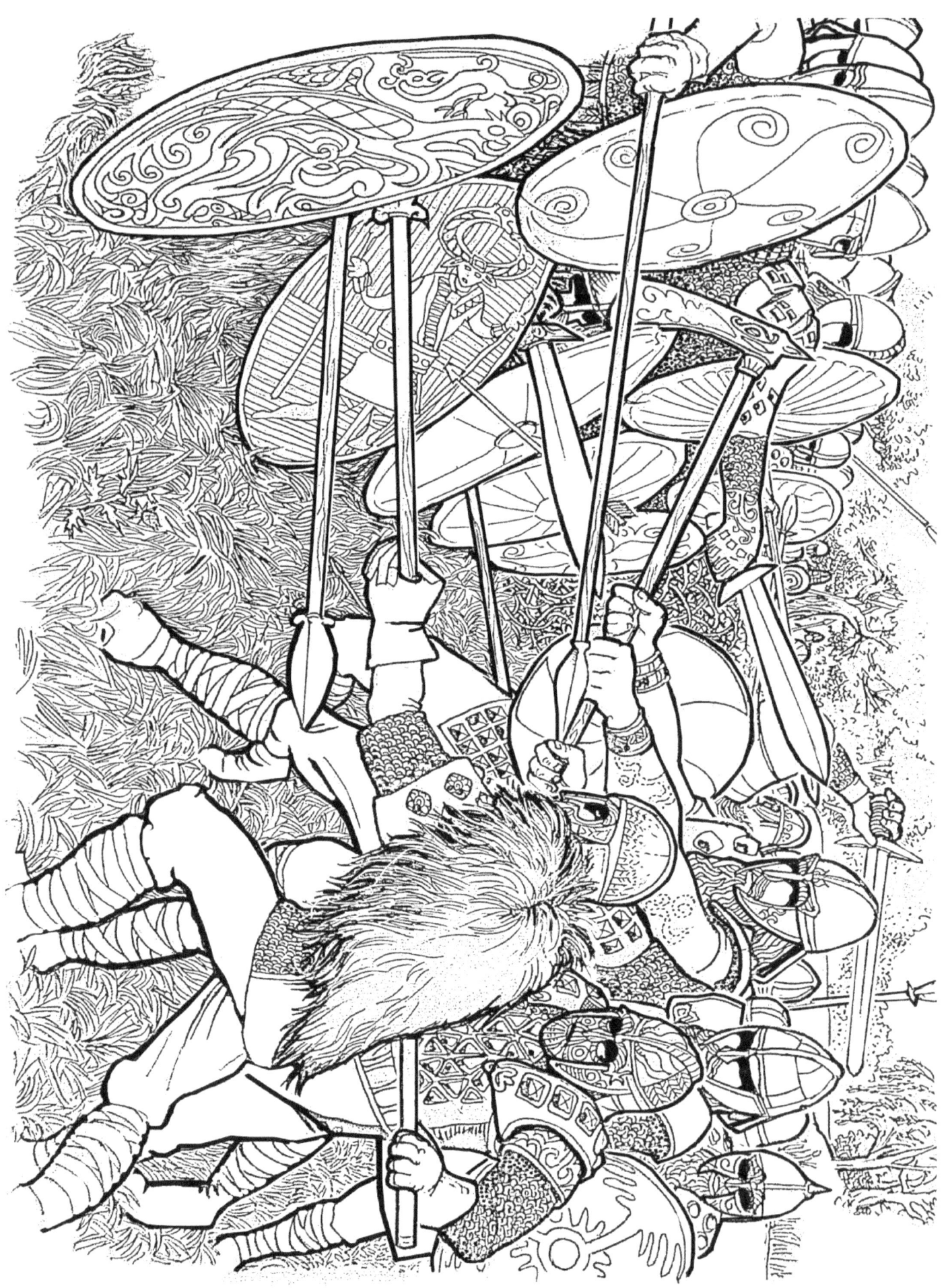

WALL OF SHIELDS

THE SHIELD WALL WAS A FEATURE OF BATTLE INTRODUCED FROM NORTHERN EUROPE BY SCANDINAVIAN INVADERS AND INCORPORATED INTO THE SAXON MARTIAL SYSTEM WITH GREAT EFFECT. IT WAS FEATURED IN THE BAYEUX TAPESTRY. IT MAY HAVE LED TO THE DEVELOPMENT OF THE FEARSOME WAR AXE. THIS WOULD BE USED TO SMASH THE WALL AND TO PRISE IT APART. THE SHIELDS WERE ESSENTIALLY USED AS A DEFENSIVE BARRICADE, BUT IN ATTACK IT WOULD PUSH ASIDE LESS ORGANISED DEFENDERS

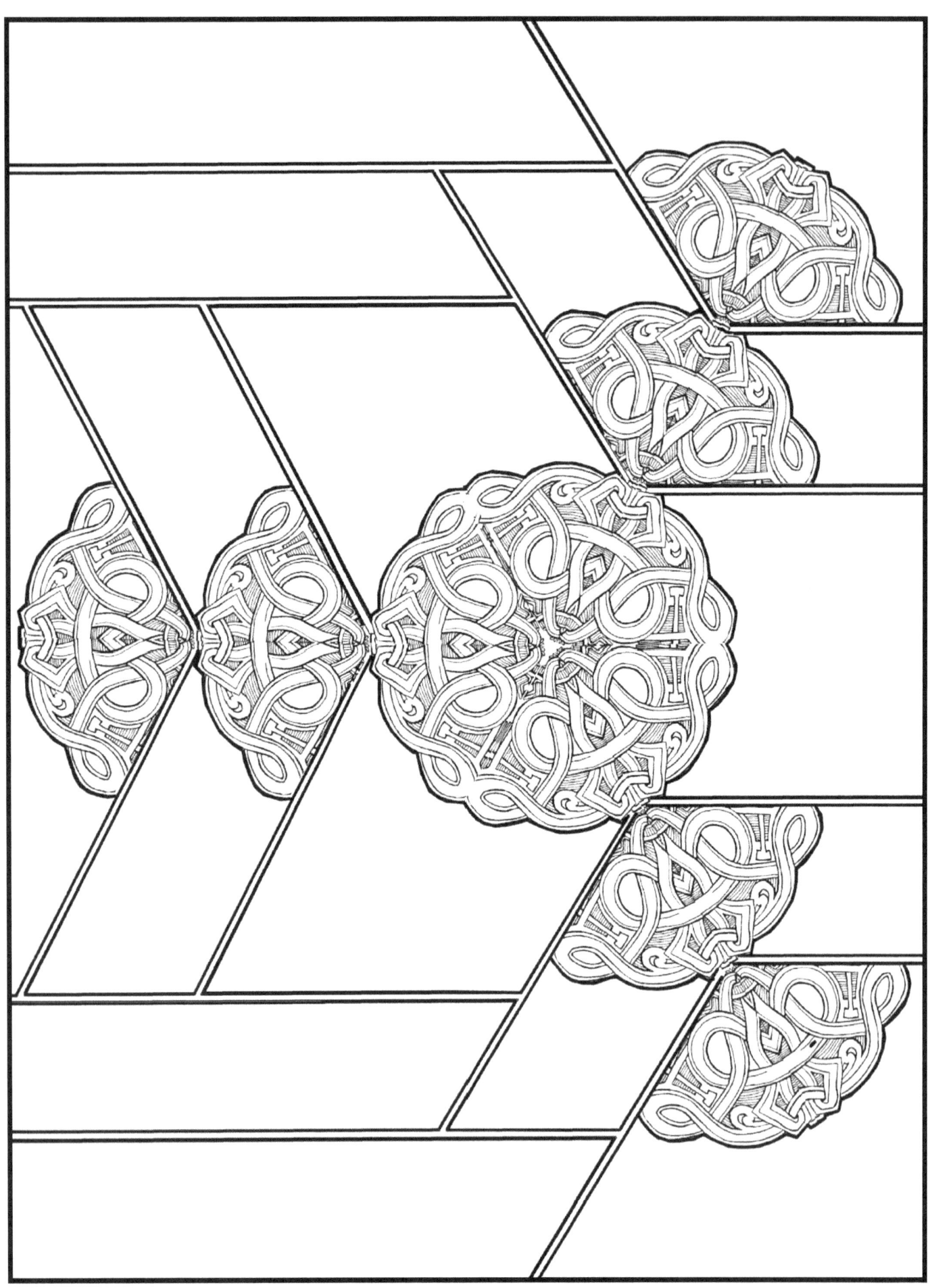

THE POWER OF THREE

THE DESIGN OF THE IMAGE IS DIVIDED INTO THREE SECTIONS. EACH SECTION IS HALVED AND MIRRORED TO CREATE A SYMMETRICAL SEGMENT. THIS IS THEN REPEATED THREE TIMES ABOUT THE CENTRAL AXIS. THIS FORM OF DECORATION REACHED A PEAK DURING THE ROMANESQUE PERIOD.

THE "BOOK OF KELLS" IS AN EXCELLENT EXAMPLE. ITS ORIGINS ARE ANCIENT AND PRE-CHRISTIAN. THE CIRCLE REPRESENTS THE EARTH AND HEAVENS TURNING. THESE NOTIONS OF THE SUN AND MOON MOVING ABOUT THE SKY PREDATE STONEHENGE.

THE ILLUMINATION ARTIST USED ALL THE COLOURS AVAILABLE TO THEM, WHICH WERE NOT AS WIDE A RANGE AS AVAILABLE TODAY. THE BLACK INK CAME FROM A GROWTH CAUSED BY AN INSECT ON OAK TREES AND DRAWN ONTO VELLUM (CALF SKIN)

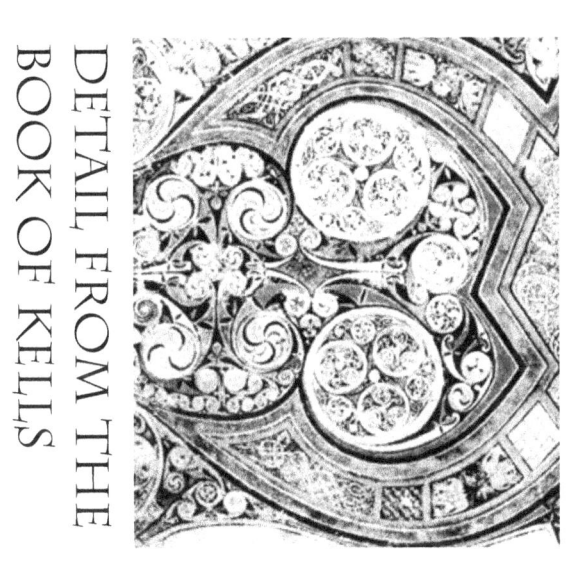

DETAIL FROM THE
BOOK OF KELLS

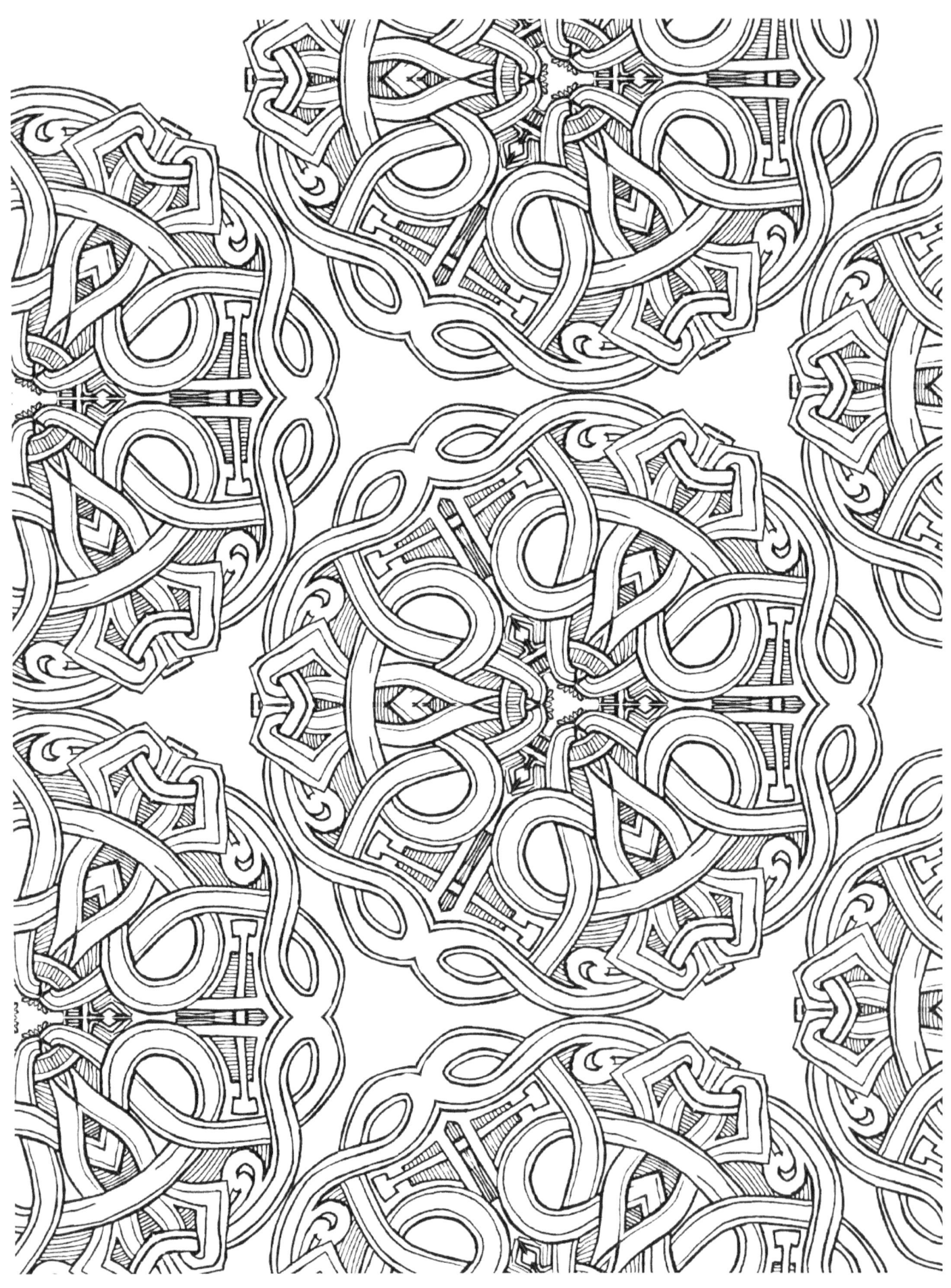

How did the artist and craftsmen and women create such intricate patterns?

I don't know, but try this

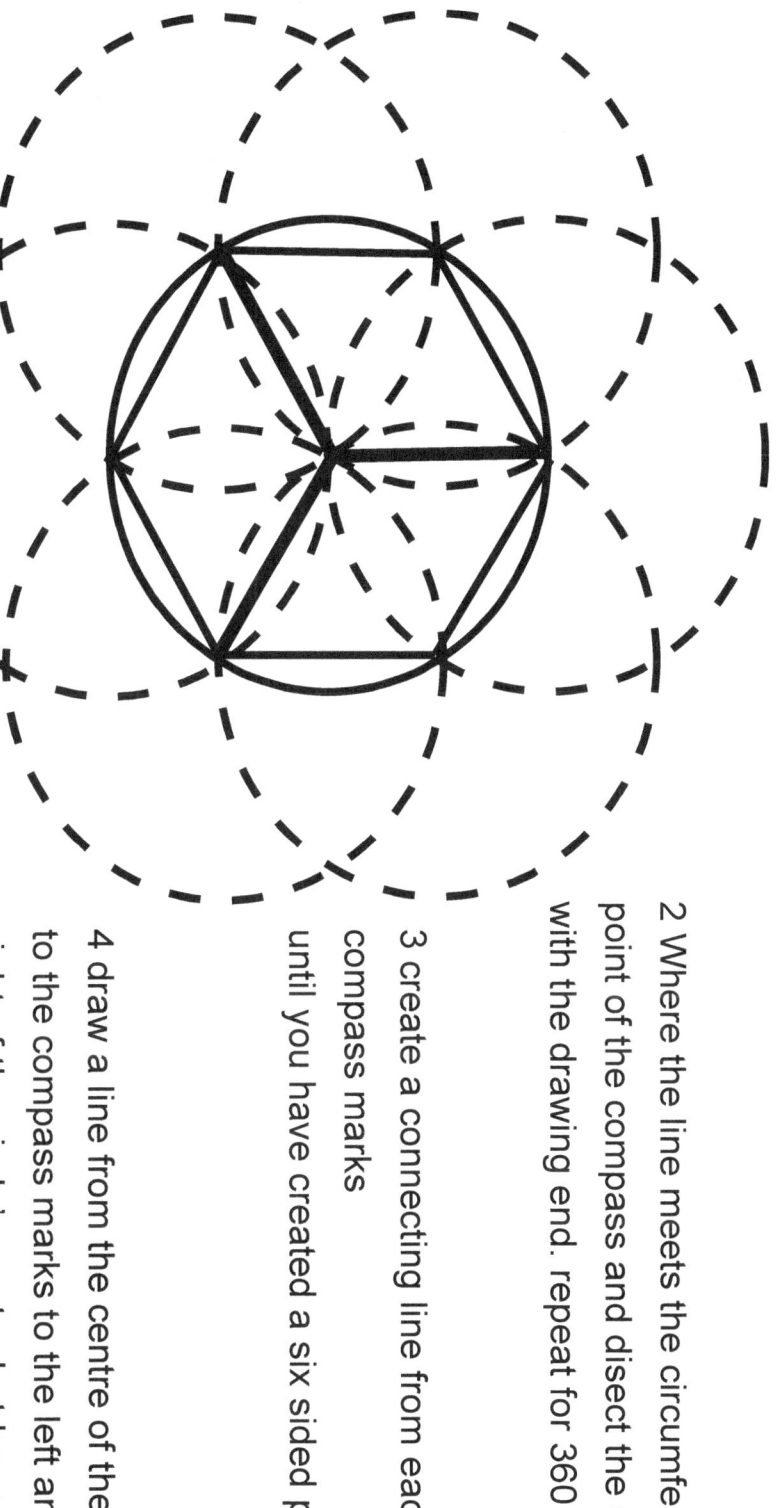

1 Using a compass, draw a circle, create a vertical line from the centre to the circumference

2 Where the line meets the circumference place the point of the compass and disect the circumference with the drawing end. repeat for 360 degrees

3 create a connecting line from each of the compass marks until you have created a six sided polygon

4 draw a line from the centre of the circle to the compass marks to the left and right of the circle's centre but beneath it

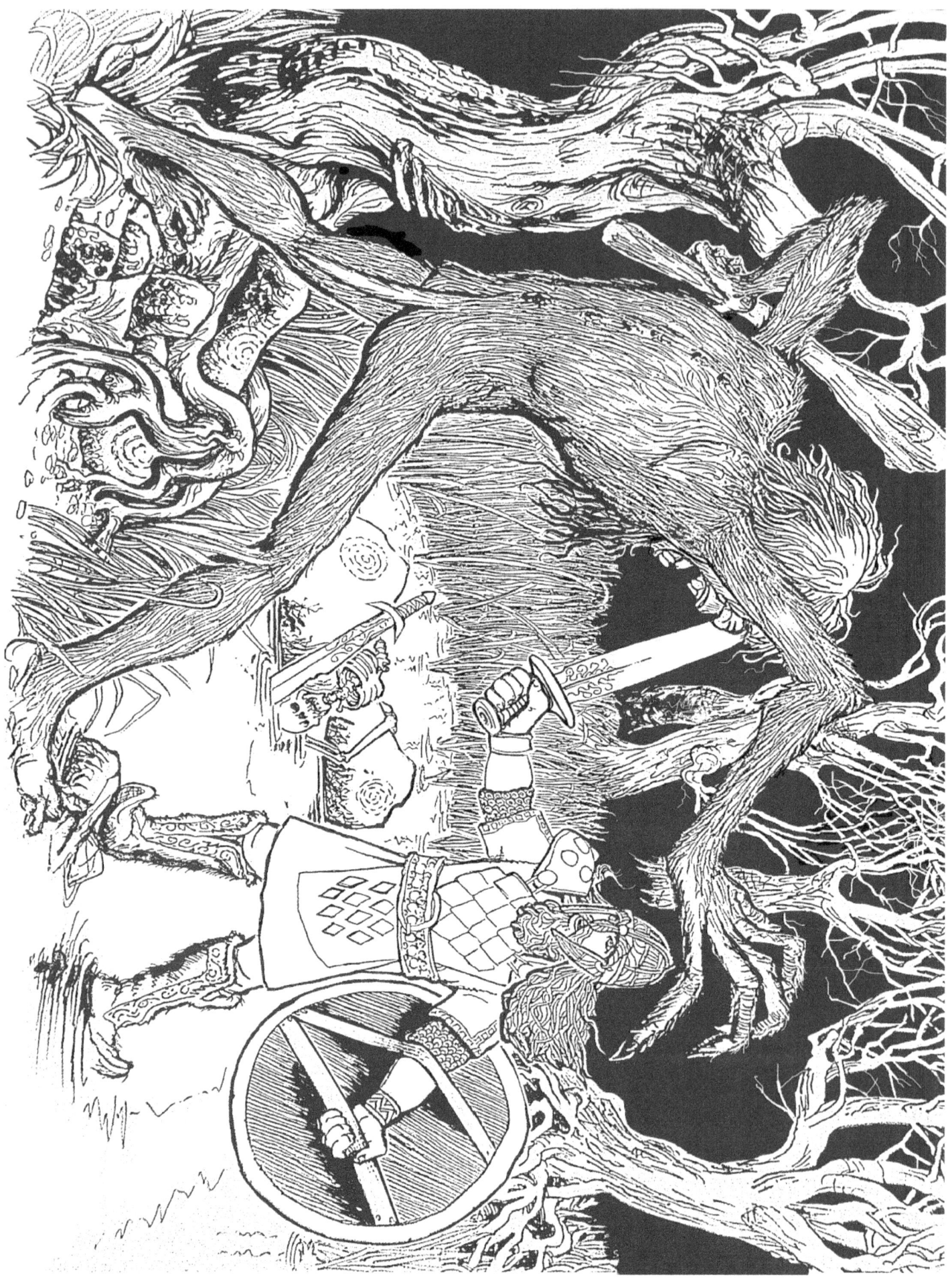

BEOWULF

BEOWULF IS AN EARLY EXAMPLE OF ENGLISH WRITING ALTHOUGH ITS GENEALOGY SHOWS IT TO BE PART OF THE NORTHERN EUROPEAN/SCANDINAVIAN ORAL TRADITION

IN THIS IMAGE BEOWULF IS CONFRONTING GRENDEL. GRENDEL IS DESCRIBED AS BEING FROM THE OFFSPRING OF CAIN AND A BEAST WHOM DWELLS IN THE FELLS. ORC IS ANGLO SAXON FOR STRANGER, SO THE FEAR OF THE ODD, UNKNOWN OR STRANGERS SHOWS THE ENCLOSED MINDSET OF THESE TIMES.

BEOWULF IS SHOWN IN HIS ARMOUR AND WEARING BOOTS AS THE SAMI PEOPLE OF NORTHERN NORWAY WEAR IN WINTER.

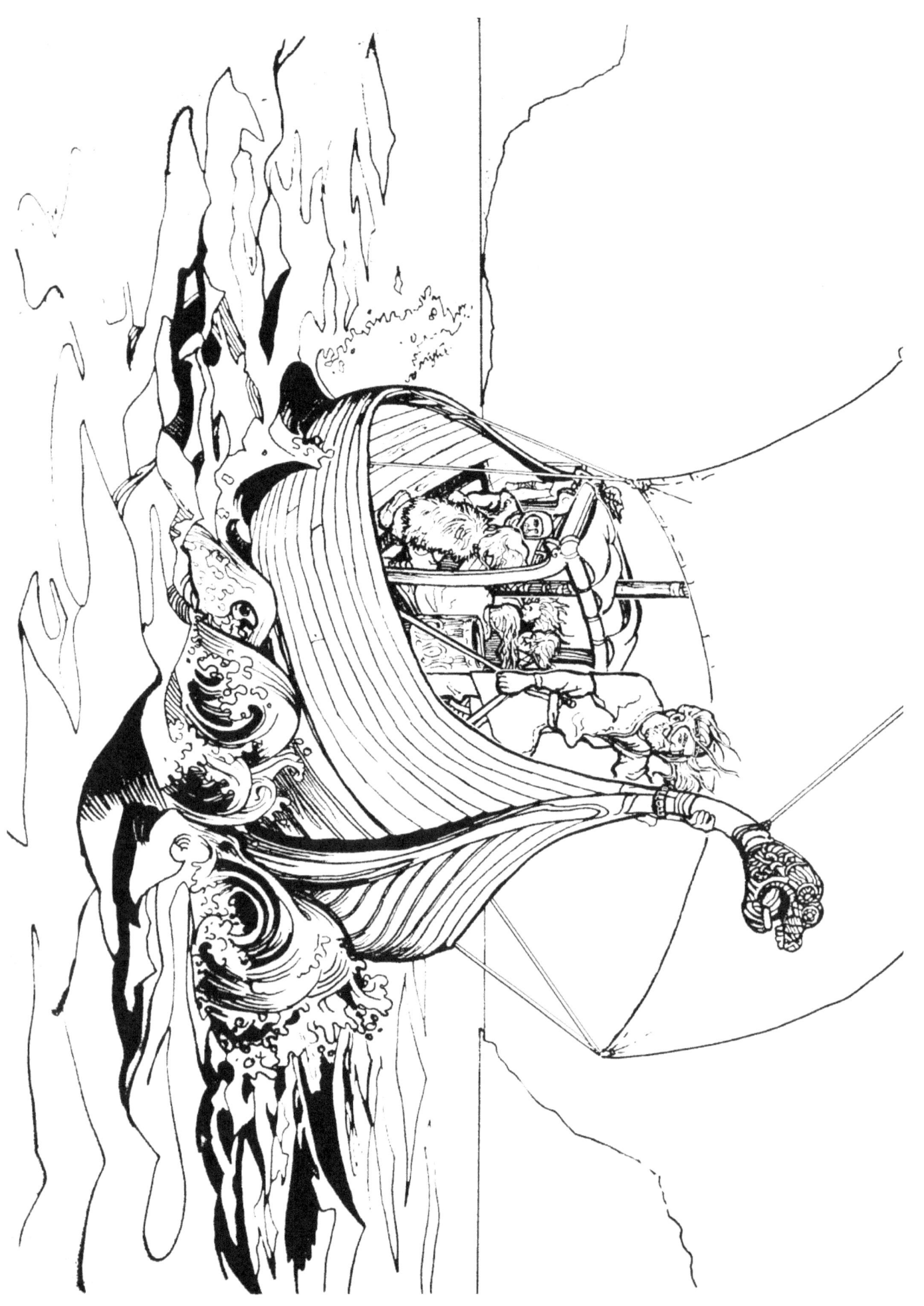

SWAN'S ROAD

THE SEAFARING FOLK FROM THE NORTH HAVE HAD AN ENORMOUS EFFECT ON THE CULTURE OF NORTHERN EUROPE. INDIRECTLY CREATING THE ENGLISH AND THE ENGLISH LANGUAGE.

THE CLINKER BUILT SHIPS THEY BUILT WERE SWIFT AND SHALLOW ENOUGH TO NAVIGATE RIVERS INTO THE HINTERLAND WHEN WAYFARING.

THIS IMAGE SHOWS A LONGSHIP. THERE ARE EXAMPLES IN MUSEUMS. THE 'HEAD' IS BASED UPON AN EXAMPLE FROM THE OSEBERG SHIP BURIAL IN OSLO UNIVERSITY WINDSWEPT FJORD SCENE, WITH A WAVE CUTTER TRAVELLING THE SALT TRAILS.

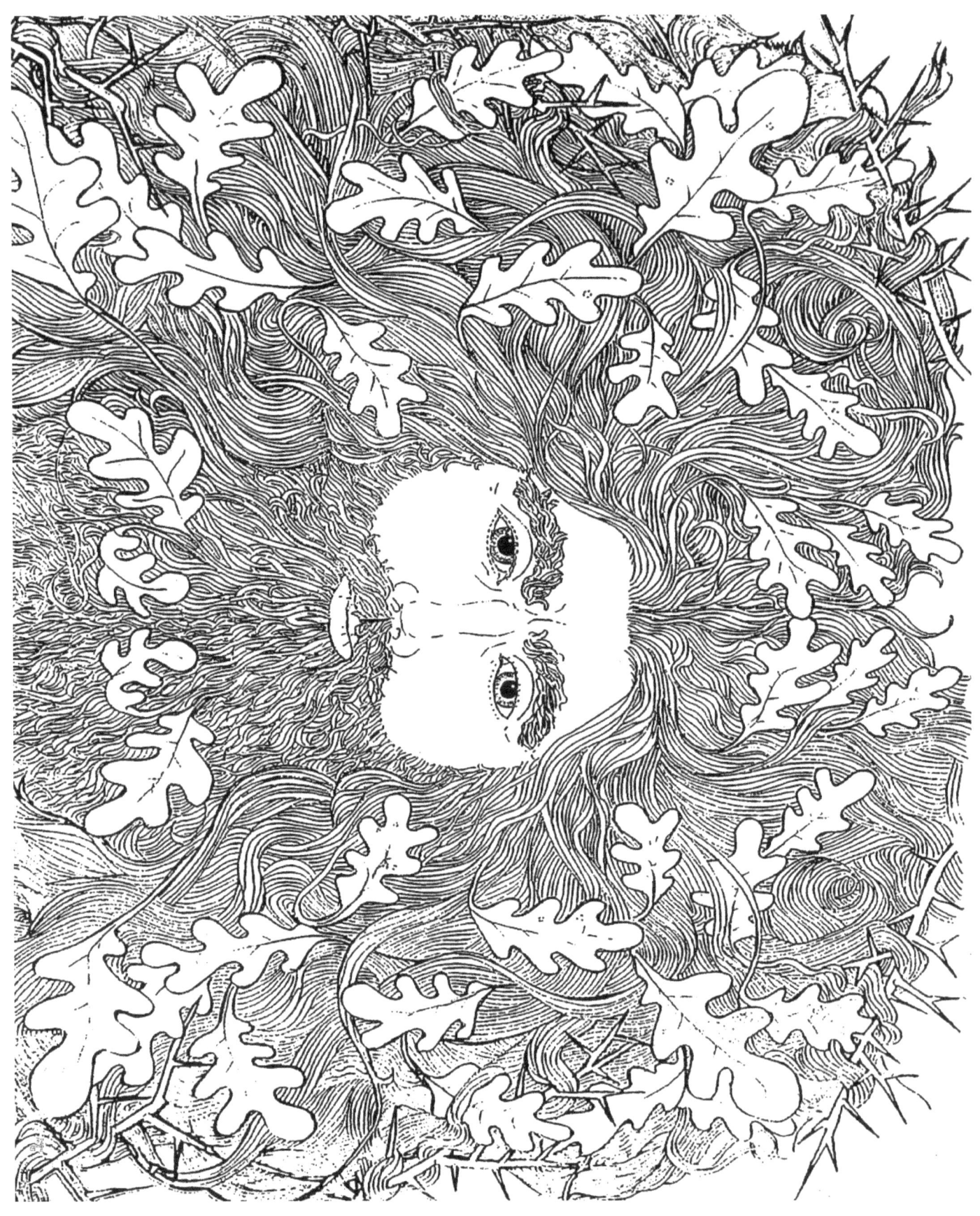

THE GREEN MAN

AN ANCIENT MYTHICAL FIGURE OFTEN DEPICTED WITH VEGETATION GROWING ORGANICALLY OUT OF HIS IMAGE. CAN STILL BE SEEN TO THIS DAY WHERE TRADITIONAL MAY DAY CELEBRATIONS ARE HELD. THE GREEN MAN IS SEEN AS A PERSONIFICATION OF NATURE AND FERTILITY HENCE THE ASSOCIATION WITH SPRING AND THE END OF WINTER.

AS MENTIONED AT THE START OF THIS COLOURING BOOK: TO GIVE DEFINITION TO THE GREENS OF THE GREEN MAN YOU COULD TRY USING SOME COMPLIMENTARY COLOURS MIXED INTO THE GREEN(S)

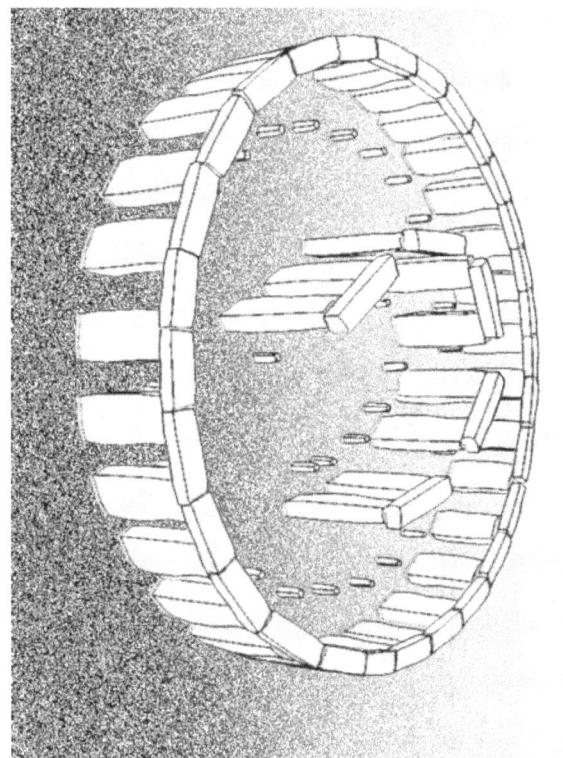

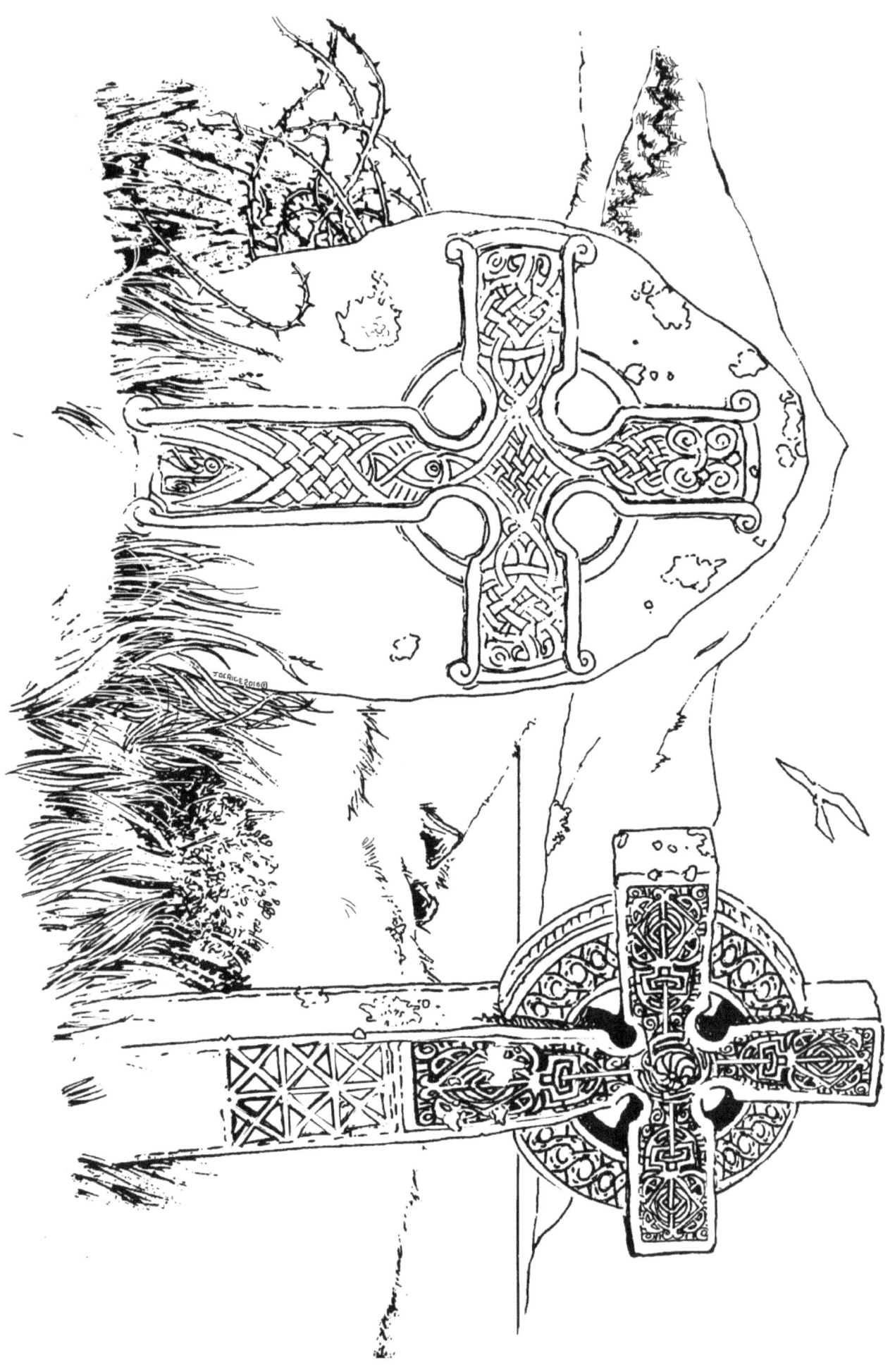

CELTIC CROSSES

CHRISTIANITY CAME TO BRITAIN DURING THE ROMAN EMPIRE'S OCCUPATION. AS THE ROMANS WITHDREW THEIR GARRISONS, THE 'BARBARIANS' TOOK ADVANTAGE OF THE WEAKNESS OF THE FORMER COLONY AND CONQUERED MOST OF WHAT IS NOW ENGLAND. THESE NORTHERN TRIBES WERE SAXONS, ANGLES, JUTES AND FRIESIANS. (MODERN DAY GERMANY AND DENMARK)

RAIDING PARTIES WOULD OFTEN TAKE THE ABLE BODIED AS SLAVES TO SELL, THE MARKET BEING THE ROMAN AND NON-ROMAN WORLD.

ST PATRICK IS A RENOWNED SLAVE TURNED MISSIONARY. THE IRISH MONASTERIES WHICH HE HELPED TO ESTABLISH, HAD LINKS WITH EARLY CHRISTIAN COMMUNITIES AROUND THE MEDITERRANEAN.

THESE EARLY MISSIONARIES PROSELYTISED IN THE PAGAN SOCIETIES OF THE SAXONS. THE PROCESS OF ABSORBING THE PAGAN ART-FORMS INTO CHRISTIAN ICONS IS OBSERVABLE IN THE CONVERSION OF PAGAN SITES INTO PLACES OF CHRISTIAN WORSHIP AND THE PLACING OF CHRISTIAN SYMBOLS ONTO NEOLITHIC STANDING STONES. THIS EVOLVED INTO THE CELTIC CROSS

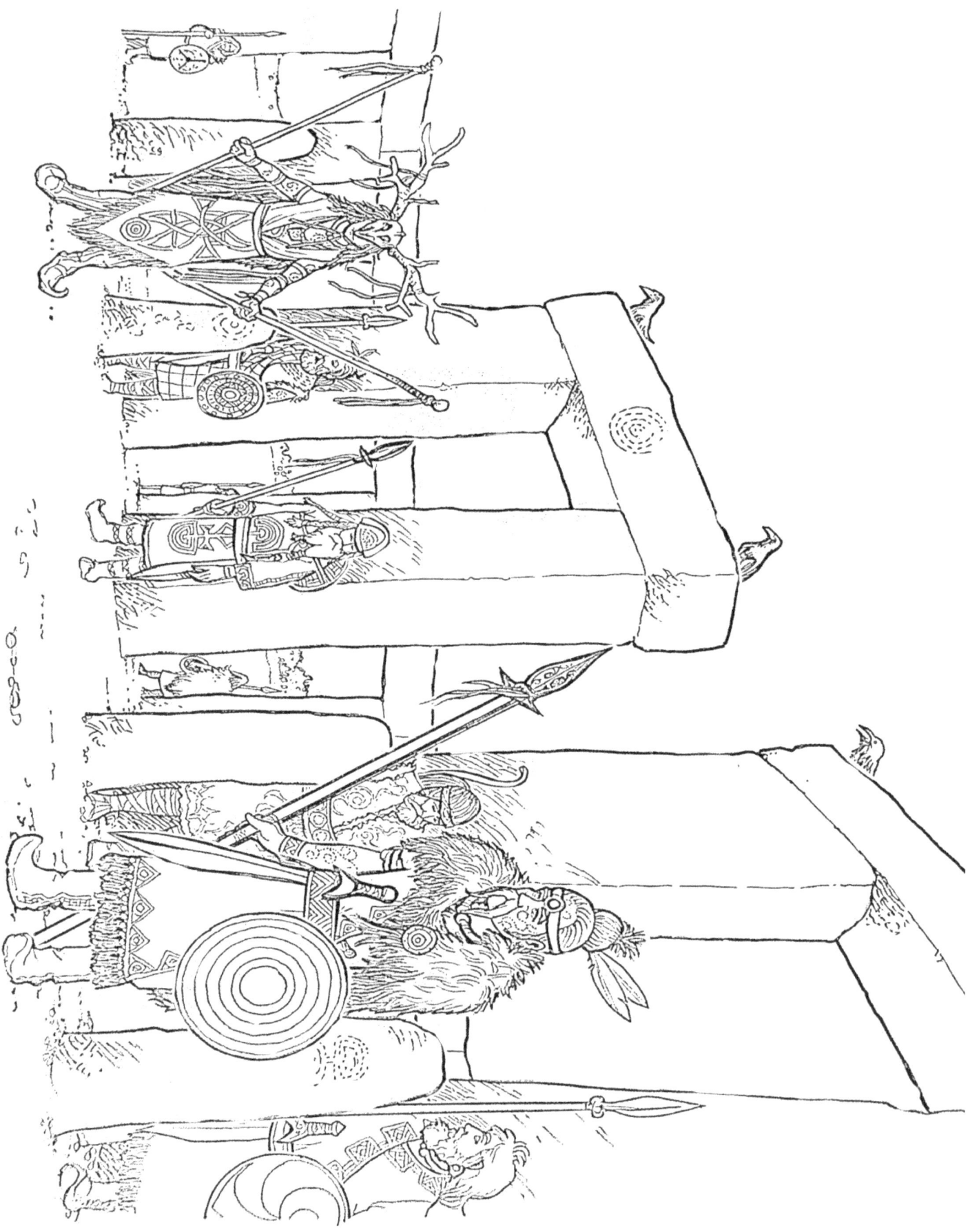

SHAMANISTIC PRACTICES

THE NEOLITHIC PEOPLES WHO CONSTRUCTED THE HENGE CELEBRATED THEIR ANCESTORS AND WERE KEENLY AWARE OF THE SEASONAL MARKER POINTS AND ITS IMPLICATION FOR GROWING FOODSTUFFS. THE IMPORTANCE OF THE END OF WINTER IS STILL IN THE BACKGROUND OF MODERN SOCIETIES WINTER FESTIVALS

STONEHENGE HAS BEEN DATED BY SCIENTISTS. THIS COLOSSAL UNDERTAKING WAS CONTEMPORARY IN ITS CONSTRUCTION TO THE BUILDING OF THE EGYPTIAN PYRAMIDS.

ALTHOUGH IT SEEMS TO HAVE DROPPED OUT OF RITUAL USE AT A TIME OF SOCIAL CHANGE, THAT COINCIDED WITH THE ARRIVAL OF THE "BEAKER" PEOPLE AND METALS.

THE IMPRESSIVE SHAPE AND DIMENSIONS OF STONEHENGE WOULD SURELY NOT HAVE BEEN IGNORED BY THE CREATORS MYTHS AND LEGENDS.

IT COULD WELL BE THE ORIGINAL INSPIRATION FOR THE LEGEND OF KING ARTHUR'S ROUND TABLE

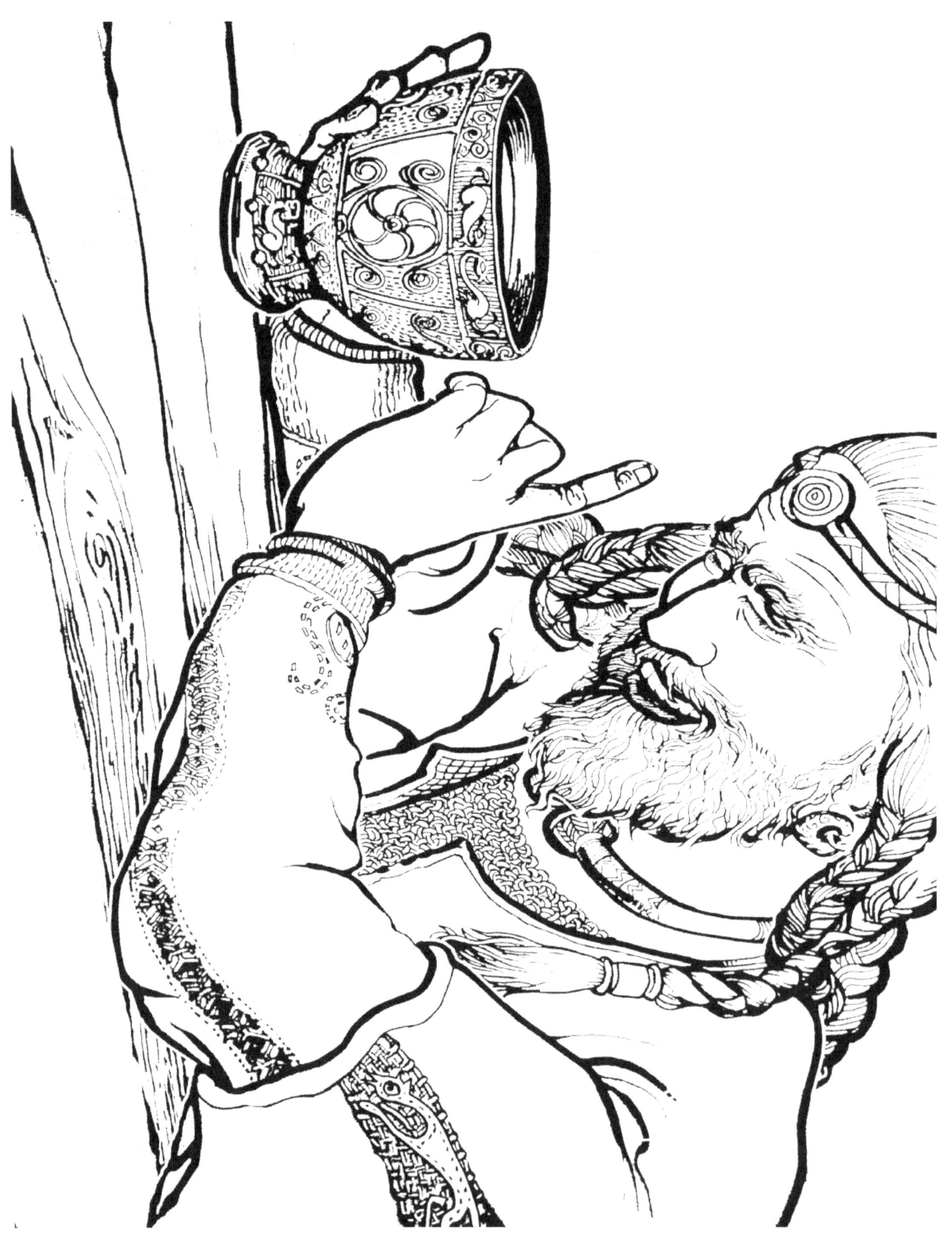

IN HIS CUPS

THE PRACTICE OF FEASTING IS A CORNERSTONE OF THE WARRIOR SOCIETY. IT WAS A DEMONSTRATION OF WEALTH AND POWER TO SHOW GENEROSITY TO FOLLOWERS.

"THERE WAS THE LAUGHTER OF HEROES, HARP-MUSIC RAN, WORDS WERE WARM-HEARTED..."

"..TO THE LAND'S GUARDIAN SHE OFFERED FIRST THE FLOWING CUP, BADE HIM BE BLITHE AT THE BEER DRINKING..."

THESE ARE A FEW OF THE REFERENCES TO FEASTING AND BANQUETS FROM "BEOWULF"

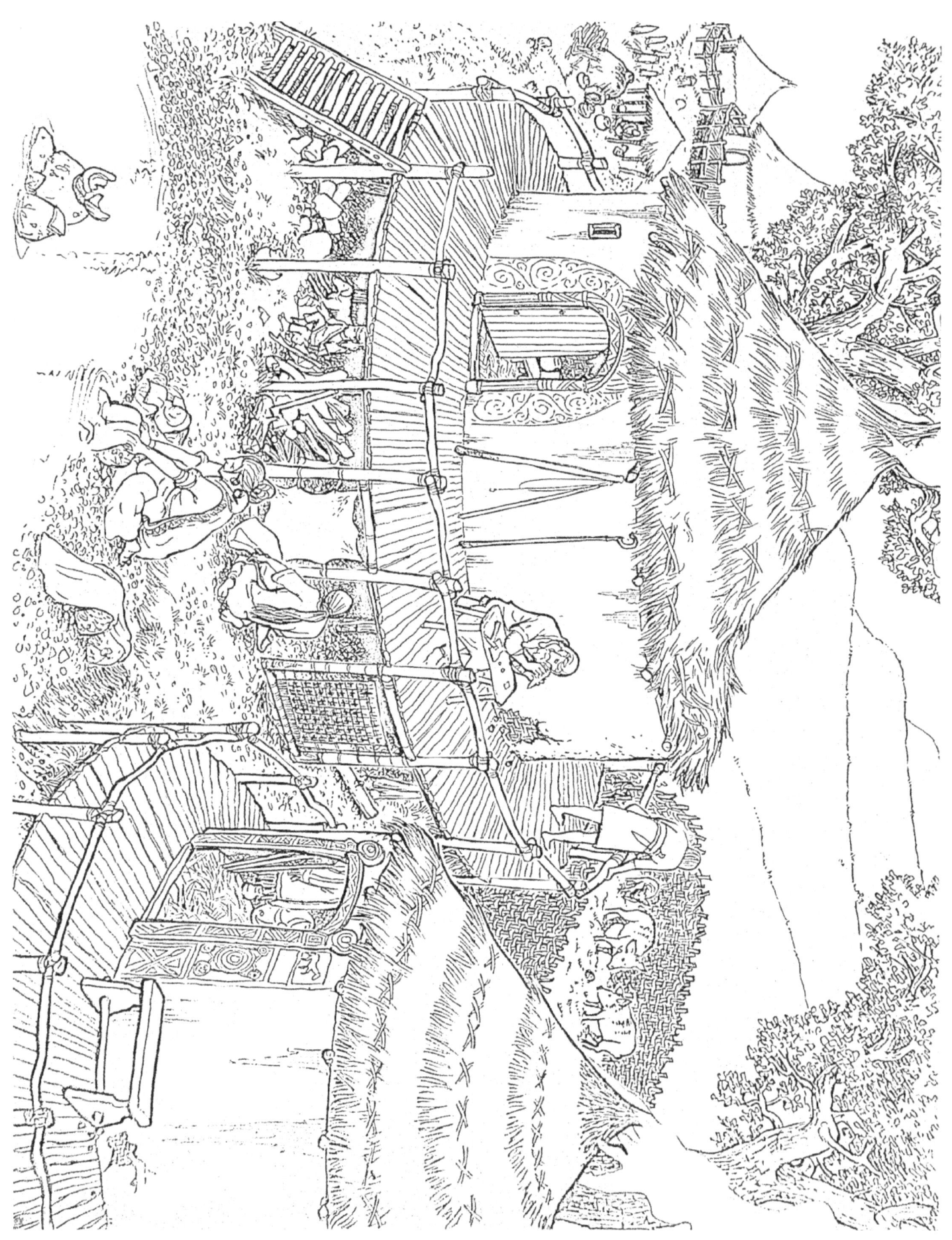

ANCIENT BRITISH VILLAGE

ROUND HOUSES HAVE BEEN PART OF THE RURAL LIFESTYLE OF
THE BRITISH ISLE FROM NEOLITHIC TIMES. THESE FORMS ARE
ASSOCIATED PRIMARILY WITH NEOLITHIC, IRON AGE AND
BRONZE AGE.
THE BASIC DESIGN IS SUITABLE FOR WATERSIDE USE ON STILTS
AND SITTING ON THE GROUND

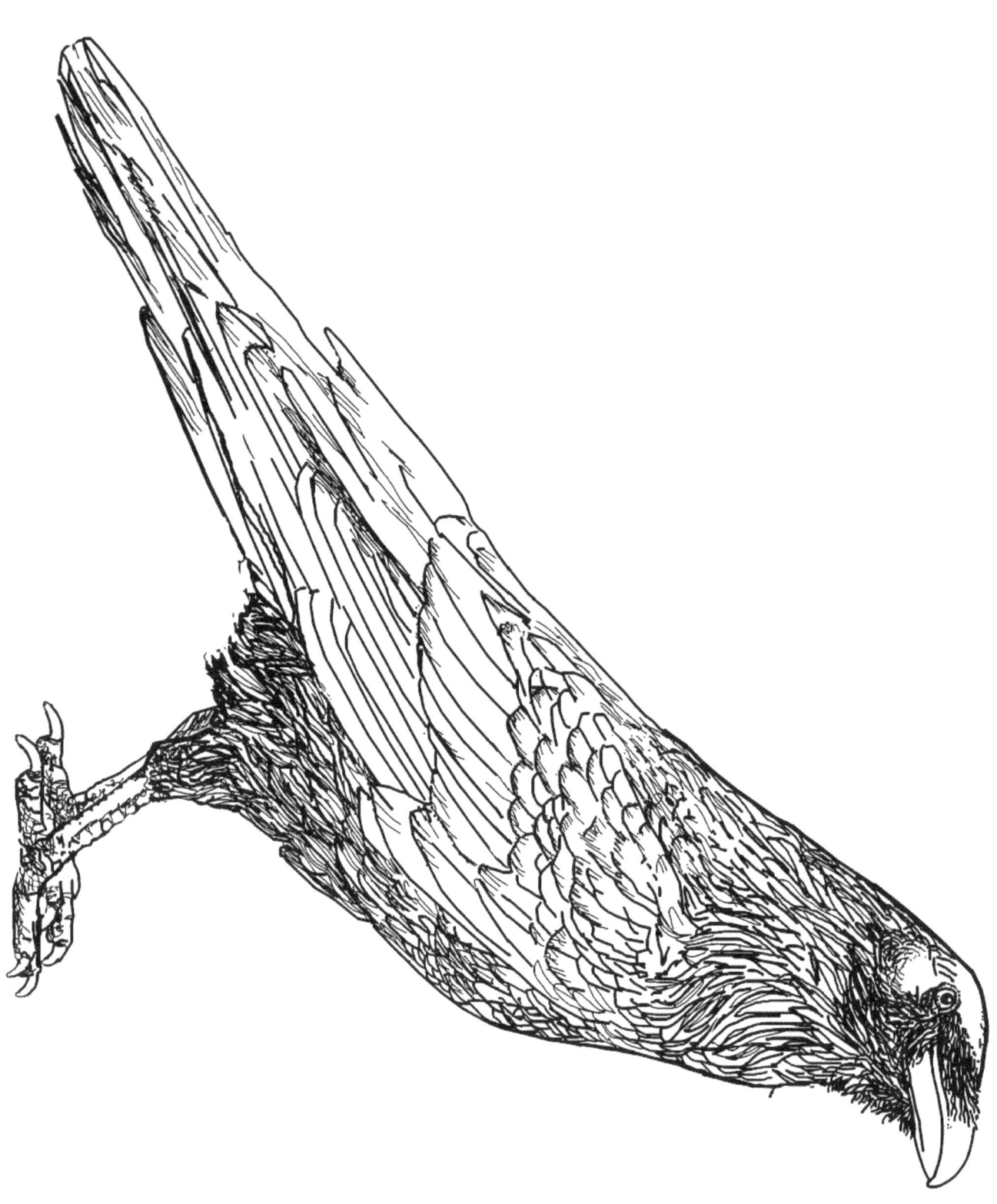

RAVENS

MESSENGERS OF THE GODS

RAVENS FEATURE IN ART AND LEGEND AS THE BIRD ASSOCIATED WITH WAR AND ITS AFTERMATH AS CARRION

SHINY BLACK
FEATHERS

www.ingramcontent.com/pod-product-compliance
Lightning Source LLC
Chambersburg PA
CBHW081135180526
45170CB00008B/3111